HISTORY OF THE KEESHOND

Approximately 15,000 years ago, man and dog first came together. Although they hunted the same game and were both mammals, the two species had little in common on the surface. Deep within each, however, the need for community existed, and that is what ultimately brought them together.

On a cold night somewhere in eastern Europe, a group of human cave dwellers were probably huddled together around a strong fire. As they dined on a recent kill, one member of a pack of wolves that had been loitering around the cave for days picking up scraps of leftover meat began to slowly approach the opening of the cave. As one of the humans noticed the bold creature looking directly at the group, he or she had the impulse to toss the animal some meat. As the wolf snatched the piece up and retreated into the darkness, the beginnings of a 4,000 year-old relationship took place.

The Keeshond's distinctive characteristics— his small pointed ears, weather-resistant double coat, and fur between toes—show him to be a close relative to the wolf.

Experts are not sure how long it took, but eventually the wolf became closer and closer to mankind. It is believed that these packs of carnivores began to follow the nomadic humans from whom they had learned to scavenge from, and eventually, the animal became semi-domesticated. Over time, these "tame" wolves began to interbreed with each other and a new species eventually formed: *Canis familiaris*, or the domestic dog.

Although the early dog's association with mankind slowly began to change its behavior, it was very wolf-like for obvious reasons. Its physical attributes began to change as well. Primitive dogs became more puppy-like than their wild cousins. Their foreheads became rounder, like a puppy's, and their teeth were smaller. They also retained some of the personality seen in wolf pups, becoming playful, subservient and dependent. This early dog even developed a new vocal technique, the bark, a sound absent from the wolf's vocabulary.

The Keeshond became popular in Holland and was recognized as its national breed.

THE SPITZ FAMILY

The Keeshond (pronounced "kayz-hawnd," with the plural Keeshonden) is a member of the Spitz family of dogs, the oldest known type of dog and a close relative of the wolf. The Keeshond can be traced back directly to the ancestors of other Spitz breeds such as the Alaskan Malamute, Siberian Husky and Samoyed.

What sets the Spitz breeds apart from other types of dogs are their distinctive, wolf-like characteristics: they have small, pointed ears that stick straight up and are less prone to frost-bite; weather-resistant double coats with an undercoat that can keep them warm in very cold climates; fur between their toes to protect their feet against rough ice; and efficient medium-sized bodies.

Where did the Spitz come from? It is believed that this distinct type of dog descended directly from primitive dogs, and had its development in the northern parts of the world. The indigenous people of the Arctic regions bonded closely with these dogs and soon became dependent on them for their very survival. Spitz dogs helped northern dwellers with hunting, herding, guarding and hauling. They also provided these people with companionship—something no doubt valued in the harsh, unforgiving environment in which they lived.

ENTER THE KEESHOND

It is not known exactly when the Keeshond departed from the other Spitz breeds and developed into its own breed, but fossil history shows that dogs resembling the Keeshond were

Also known as the Dutch Barge Dog, the Keeshond was brought to England in 1905 and recognized by the Kennel Club in 1925.

prevalent several thousand years ago in what is now the Netherlands.

Experts believe that the Spitz breeds migrated from the north with their human companions and settled in various parts of Europe, as well as other continents. The Spitz developed into a variety of different groups, each known for the part of the continent where it had settled. From one of these groups, a breed known as the German Wolfspitz developed and is considered one and the same with the Keeshond.

The Keeshond became popular in Holland and was recognized as its national breed. It even appeared on an early seal created during the Middle Ages bearing a scene depicting the founding of Amsterdam. To this day, the breed is synonymous with Holland.

Because much of Holland is below sea level and crossed by drainage canals, rivers and man-made waterways, occupations such as boatman and barge runner were common ways to earn a living in the days before the Industrial Revolution. More often than not, at least one Keeshond was kept on each ship to serve as a watchdog and companion. Eventually, the breed became known as the Dutch Barge Dog.

While Dutch history immortalized the Keeshond, the country's political strife in the

18th century nearly destroyed the breed. At the time of the French Revolution, the Keeshond became associated with the common people of Holland, known as the patriots. The leader of this movement, a man named Cornelius de Ghyselaer, owned a Keeshond. The dog was his constant companion and de Ghyselaer was rarely seen without him. In fact, de Ghyselaer became so closely associated with the breed that it is believed the breed's name came from him. According to theory, the Keeshond, which was then known as the Wolfspitz, acquired its modern name from the man, whose nickname was "Keez," and who belonged to a political party called "Kezen."

The Keeshond achieved the height of its popularity during this time period. When de Ghyselaer was killed by opposing forces, his political party fell by the wayside and the Keeshond was suddenly in grave danger of dying out. It became a hazard to own one of these dogs, and many were destroyed. If the people of rural Netherlands had not continued to love and care for the breed, it would not be alive today.

Not long after its acceptance by the Kennel Club of England, the breed's name was officially changed to Keeshond in honor of Cornelius de Ghyselaer, whose nickname was "Keez." He was a strong supporter and promoter of the breed.

A similar dog to the one first seen with Dutch seamen hundreds of years before, the Keeshond was officially recognized in the US by the American Kennel Club in 1930.

After its near demise, the Keeshond lived a relatively quiet, isolated life in the Netherlands. Then one day, in 1905, a young English woman named Gwendolyn Hamilton-Fletcher discovered the breed while on vacation in Holland with her parents. She brought two young dogs back with her on her return to Great Britain, where the dog breeding gentry of the time took notice of the breed. Later, after Gwendolyn married, she imported more Keeshonden into England, and was instrumental in getting the breed recognized by the Kennel Club, England's purebred dog registry.

The Dutch Barge Dog became an accepted Kennel Club breed in 1925, and was recognized in a variety of colors: white, black, silver-gray and cream. Not long after, the breed's name was officially changed to the Keeshond. This was most likely done in honor of Cornelius de Ghyselaer who was so closely associated with the breed's history.

THE KEESHOND IN AMERICA

The breed eventually found its way to America and a small group of dedicated fanciers worked for American Kennel Club recognition of the Keeshond. In 1930, the Keeshond was officially recognized in the United States by the American Kennel Club, and it was a very similar dog to the one first seen accompanying Dutch seamen on their ships hundreds of years before. The silver-gray color was the only one accepted in the breed, and while this color is the only one allowed in the show

Profuse and thick, the Keeshond's coat was designed not for appearance, but to keep the dog warm in cold temperatures.

ring, dogs with coats bearing the other original Keeshond colors are sometimes produced in litters from gray-colored parents.

Even though the breed was developed in Europe, the Keeshond enjoys its greatest popularity here in the United States. The United States currently boasts the largest population of Keeshonden of any country in the world. The breed currently ranks 50th in popularity among the American Kennel Club's 141 breeds. This is a comfortable ranking that indicates some popularity, but not so much that the Keeshond is in danger of being "overbred," a situation that can result in harm to the breed.

The Keeshond is a member of the American Kennel Club's non-sporting group, a categorization for dogs bred primarily as companions. Two national clubs exist to promote the welfare of the Keeshond; the Keeshond Club of America, and the American Keeshond Society.

DESCRIPTION OF THE KEESHOND

The Keeshond is a medium-sized dog that weighs approximately 40 pounds and should measure 17 to 18 inches at the shoulder. His body is short-coupled and square in appearance and he has dark, almond-shaped eyes.

One of the Keeshond's most attractive features is his coat. Profuse and thick, the Keeshond coat was designed to not only look good, but to keep the dog warm in cold temperatures. Because of this function, the Keeshond coat contains what is known as a double-coat; a layer of soft, fuzzy hair underneath longer guard hairs that protrude away from the skin. As a result of this double coat, the Keeshond is a breed that sheds regularly. People who live with a Keeshond have to accept the fact that there will be dog hair around the house. While regular grooming and frequent vacuuming can help reduce the amount of loose hair on the carpet, there is no way to completely eliminate dog hair in the home of a Keeshond.

Alert and intelligent, the Keeshond's expression is a distinctive characteristic of the breed.

Keeshond breeders place much emphasis on the dog's expression. Considered a distinctive characteristic of this breed, correct expression is one of alertness and intelligence. It is created by the combination of "spectacles" (a dark line encircling the eye), obliquely set eyes and well-placed ears.

When it comes to temperament, the Keeshond is, above all else, a family dog. Because of his long history as a companion dog, there is nothing more important to a Keeshond than having a family who loves him and spends a lot of time with him. A Keeshond cannot cope with being chained out in the yard for hours on end, condemned to a life of isolation. The breed thrives on human companionship and cannot function well without it.

Thanks to his long history in the Netherlands as a guard dog, the Keeshond is a very capable watchdog in the home. It is a vocal dog that will readily sound

The Keeshond attracts attention not only with his unique coloration, but also with his stand-off coat.

BREED STANDARD

General Appearance—The Keeshond (pronounced *kayz-hawnd*) is a natural, handsome dog of well-balanced, short-coupled body, attracting attention not only by his coloration, alert carriage, and intelligent expression, but also by his stand-off coat, his richly plumed tail well curled over his back, his foxlike expression, and his small pointed ears. His coat is very thick around the neck, fore part of the shoulders and chest, forming a lion-like ruff—more profuse in the male. His rump and hind legs, down to the hocks, are also thickly coated, forming the characteristic "trousers." His head, ears, and lower legs are covered with thick, short hair.

Size, Proportion, Substance— The Keeshond is a medium-sized, square-appearing, sturdy dog, neither coarse nor lightly made. The ideal height of fully matured dogs when measured from top of withers to the ground is 18 inches for males and 17 inches for bitches—a one inch variance either way is acceptable. While correct size is very important, it should not outweigh that for type.

Head—*Expression—* Expression is largely dependent on the distinctive character called

The Keeshond has a distinctively thick coat that forms a lion-like ruff and a richly plumed tail.

The Keeshond has a wedge-shaped head with dark eyes and triangular-shaped ears.

"spectacles"—a combination of markings and shadings in the orbital area which must include a delicate, dark line slanting from the outer corner of each eye toward the lower corner of each ear coupled with extensive eyebrows. Markings (or shadings) on face and head must present a pleasing appearance, imparting to the dog an alert and intelligent expression. **Very Serious Fault:** Absence of dark lines which form the "spectacles."

Eyes—Eyes should be dark brown in color, of medium size, almond shaped, set obliquely and neither too wide apart nor too close together. Eye rims are black.

Faults: Round and/or protruding eyes or eyes light of color.

Ears—Ears should be small, triangular in shape, mounted high on head and carried erect. Size should be proportionate to the head—length approximating the distance from the outer corner of the eye to the nearest edge of the ear. **Fault:** Ears not carried erect when at attention.

Skull—The head should be well-proportioned to the body and wedge-shaped when viewed from above—not only the muzzle, but the whole head should give this impression when the ears are drawn back by covering the nape of the neck and the ears with one hand. Head in profile should exhibit a definite stop. **Faults:** Apple head or absence of stop.

Muzzle—Of medium length, neither coarse nor snipey, and well proportioned to the skull.

Mouth—The mouth should be neither overshot nor undershot. Lips should be black and closely meeting—not thick, coarse or sagging—and with no wrinkle at the corner of the mouth. **Faults:** Overshot, undershot or wry mouth.

Teeth—The teeth should be white, sound and strong meeting in a scissors bite. **Fault:** Misaligned teeth.

Neck, Topline, Body—The ***neck*** should be moderately long,

The Keeshond's muzzle should be of medium length, well proportioned to the skull and neither coarse nor snipey.

well-shaped and well set on shoulders. The body should be compact with a short, straight back sloping slightly downward toward the hindquarters: well ribbed, barrel well rounded, short in loin, belly moderately tucked up, deep and strong of chest.

Tail —The tail should be moderately long and well feathered, set on high and tightly curled over the back. It should lie flat and close to the body. The tail must form a part of the "silhouette" of the dog's body, rather than give the appearance of an appendage.

Fault: Tail not lying close to the back.

Forequarters—Forelegs should be straight seen from any angle. Pasterns are strong with a slight slope. Legs must be of good bone in proportion to the overall dog. Shoulder to upper arm angulation is between slight to moderate.

A naturally handsome dog, the Keeshond is well balanced with a short coupled body, alert carriage and intelligent expression.

Hindquarters—Angulation in rear should be between slight to moderate to complement the fore-quarters, creating balance and typical gait. Hindquarters are well muscled with hocks perpendicular to the ground.

Feet—The feet should be compact, well rounded, catlike. Toes are nicely arched, with black nails.

Coat—The body should be abundantly covered with long, straight, harsh hair standing well out from a thick, downy undercoat. Head, including muzzle, skull and ears, should be covered with smooth, soft, short hair—velvety in texture on the ears. The neck is covered with a mane—more profuse in the male—sweeping from under the jaw and covering the whole of the front part of the shoulders and chest, as well as the top part of the shoulders. The hair on the legs should be smooth and short, except for the feathering on the front legs and "trousers" on the hind legs. Hind legs should be profusely feathered down to the hocks—not below. The hair on the tail should form a rich plume. Coat must not part down the back. The Keeshond is to be shown in a natural state with trimming permissible only on feet, pasterns, hocks and—if desired—whiskers. TRIMMING OTHER THAN AS DESCRIBED TO BE SEVERELY PENALIZED. **Faults:** Silky, wavy, or curly coats. Part in coat down the back.

Color and Markings—A dramatically marked dog, the Keeshond is a mixture of gray, black and cream. This coloration may vary from light to dark. The hair of the outer coat is black

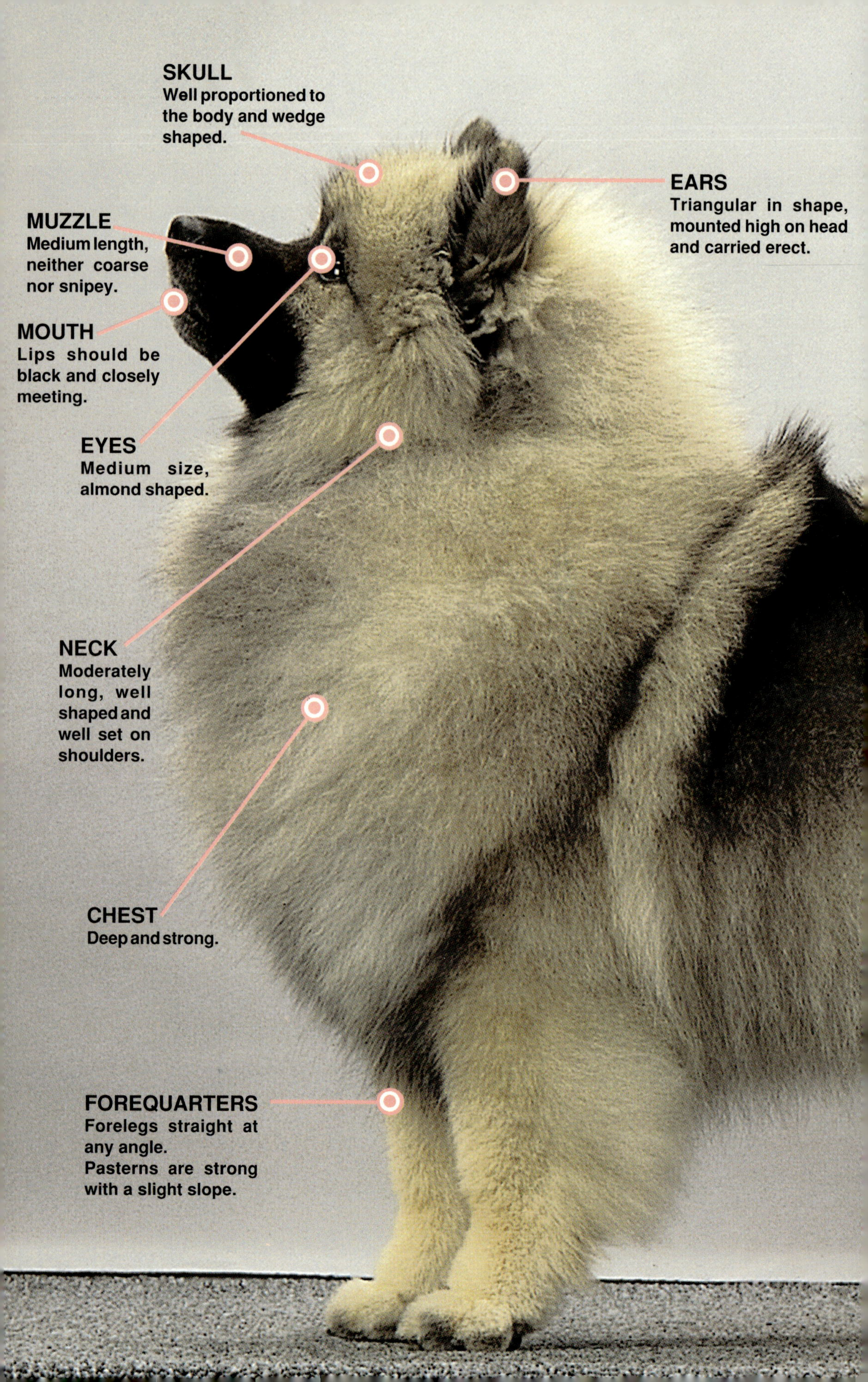
SKULL
Well proportioned to the body and wedge shaped.
EARS
Triangular in shape, mounted high on head and carried erect.
MUZZLE
Medium length, neither coarse nor snipey.
MOUTH
Lips should be black and closely meeting.
EYES
Medium size, almond shaped.
NECK
Moderately long, well shaped and well set on shoulders.
CHEST
Deep and strong.
FOREQUARTERS
Forelegs straight at any angle.
Pasterns are strong with a slight slope.

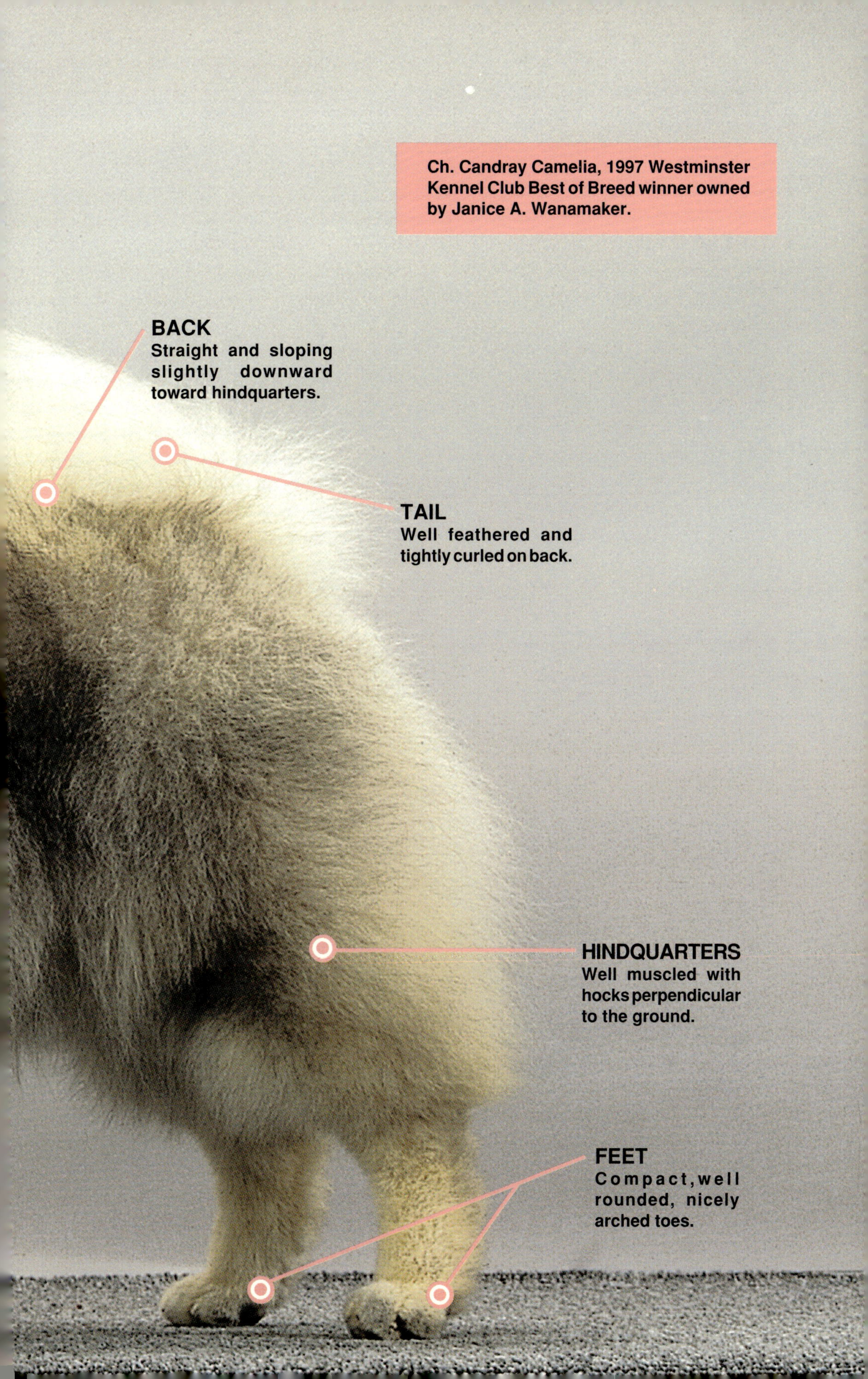

Ch. Candray Camelia, 1997 Westminster Kennel Club Best of Breed winner owned by Janice A. Wanamaker.

YOUR NEW KEESHOND PUPPY

SELECTION

When you do pick out a Keeshond puppy as a pet, don't be hasty; the longer you study puppies, the better you will understand them. Make it your transcendent concern to select only one that radiates good health and spirit and is lively on his feet, whose eyes are bright, whose coat shines, and who comes forward eagerly to make and to cultivate your acquaintance. Don't fall for any shy little darling that wants to retreat to his bed or his box, or plays coy behind other puppies or people, or hides his head under your arm or jacket appealing to your protective instinct. *Pick the Keeshond puppy who forthrightly picks you! The feeling of attraction should be mutual!*

Picking the perfect puppy will take time and patience. Looking at these three, how could you decide on just one?

DOCUMENTS

Now, a little paper work is in order. When you purchase a purebred Keeshond puppy, you should receive a transfer of ownership, registration material, and other "papers" (a list of the immunization shots, if any, the puppy may have been given; a note on whether or not the puppy has been wormed; a diet and feeding schedule to which the puppy is accustomed) and you are welcomed as a fellow owner to a long, pleasant association with a most lovable pet, and more (news)paper work.

When choosing a Keeshond pup, remember you are making a major decision. These pups will need tender love and care as well as guidance and training.

GENERAL PREPARATION

You have chosen to own a particular Keeshond puppy. You have chosen it very carefully over all other breeds and all other puppies. So before you ever get that Keeshond puppy home, you will have prepared for its arrival by reading everything you can get your hands on having to do with the management of Keeshonds and puppies. True, you will run into many conflicting opinions, but at least you will not be starting "blind." Read, study, digest. Talk over your plans with your veterinarian, other "Keeshond people," and the seller of your Keeshond puppy.

When you get your Keeshond puppy, you will find that your reading and study are far from finished. You've just scratched the surface in your plan to provide the greatest possible comfort and health for your Keeshond; and, by the same token, you do want to assure yourself of the greatest possible enjoyment of this wonderful creature. You must be ready for this puppy mentally as well as in the physical requirements.

When bringing a Keeshond into your home, allow your new puppy to become familiar with his surroundings.

A Keeshond pup needs a responsible owner to bloom into a well-rounded and trustworthy dog.

TRANSPORTATION

If you take the puppy home by car, protect him from drafts, particularly in cold weather. Wrapped in a towel and carried in the arms or lap of a passenger, the Keeshond puppy will usually make the trip without mishap. If the pup starts to drool and to squirm, stop the car for a few minutes. Have newspapers handy in case of car-sickness. A covered

On his first night in his new home your Keeshond pup may miss his mother and littermates. Soothe and comfort him to make him feel safe and secure.

carton lined with newspapers provides protection for puppy and car, if you are driving alone. Avoid excitement and unnecessary handling of the puppy on arrival. A Keeshond puppy is a very small "package" to be making a complete change of surroundings and company, and he needs frequent rest and refreshment to renew his vitality.

THE FIRST DAY AND NIGHT

When your Keeshond puppy arrives in your home, put him down on the floor and don't pick him up again, except when it is absolutely necessary. He is a dog, a real dog, and must not be lugged around like a rag doll. Handle him as little as possible, and permit no one to pick him up and baby him. To repeat, *put your Keeshond puppy on the floor or the ground and let him stay there except when it may be necessary to do otherwise.*

Quite possibly your Keeshond puppy will be afraid for a while in his new surroundings, without his mother and littermates. Comfort him and reassure him, but don't console him. Don't give him the "oh-you-poor-itsy-bitsy-puppy" treatment. Be calm, friendly, and reassuring. Encourage him to

Calm, friendly and reassuring is the best demeanor to exhibit to your new Keeshond.

walk around and sniff over his new home. If it's dark, put on the lights. Let him roam for a few minutes while you and everyone else concerned sit quietly or go about your routine business. Let the puppy come back to you.

Playmates may cause an immediate problem if the new Keeshond puppy is to be greeted by children or other pets. If not, you can skip this subject. The natural affinity between puppies and children calls for some supervision until a live-and-let-live relationship is established. This applies particularly to a Christmas puppy, when there is more excitement than usual and more chance for a puppy to swallow something upsetting. It is a better plan to welcome the puppy several days before or after the holiday week. Like a baby, your Keeshond puppy needs much rest and should not be over-handled. Once a child realizes that a puppy has "feelings" similar to his own, and can readily be hurt or injured, the opportunities for play and responsibilities provide exercise and training for both.

For his first night with you, he should be put where he is to sleep every night—say in the kitchen, since its floor can usually be easily cleaned. Let him explore the kitchen to his heart's content; close doors to confine him there. Prepare his food and feed him lightly the first night. Give him a pan with some water in it—not a lot, since most puppies will try to drink the whole pan dry. Give him an old coat or shirt to lie on. Since a coat or shirt will be strong in human scent, he will pick it out to lie on, thus furthering his feeling of security in the room where he has just been fed.

HOUSEBREAKING HELPS

Now, sooner or later—mostly sooner—your new Keeshond puppy is going to "puddle" on the floor. First take a newspaper and lay it on the puddle until the urine is soaked up onto the paper. *Save this paper.* Now take a cloth with soap and water, wipe up the floor and dry it well. Then take the wet paper and place it on a fairly large square of newspapers in a convenient corner. When cleaning up, always keep a piece

chew stems from the instinct for tooth cleaning, gum massage, and jaw exercise—plus the need for an outlet for periodic doggie tensions.

This is why dogs, especially puppies and young dogs, will often destroy property worth hundreds of dollars when their chewing instinct is not diverted from their owner's possessions. And this is why you should provide your Keeshond with something to chew—something that has the necessary functional qualities, is desirable from the Keeshond's viewpoint, and is safe for him.

It is very important that your Keeshond not be permitted to chew on anything he can break or on any indigestible thing from which he can bite sizable chunks. Sharp pieces, such as from a bone which can be broken by a dog, may pierce the intestinal wall and kill. Indigestible things that can be bitten off in chunks, such as from shoes or rubber or plastic toys, may cause an intestinal stoppage (if not regurgitated) and bring painful death, unless surgery is promptly performed.

Strong natural bones, such as 4- to 8-inch lengths of round shin bone from mature beef—either the kind you can get from a butcher or one of the variety available commercially in pet stores—may serve your Keeshond's teething needs if his mouth is large enough to handle them effectively. You may be tempted to give your Keeshond puppy a smaller bone and he may not be able to break it when you do, but puppies grow rapidly and the power of their jaws constantly increases until maturity. This means that a growing Keeshond may break one of the smaller bones at any time,

Carrots are rich in fiber, carbohydrates, and vitamin A. The CarrotBone™ by Nylabone® is a durable chew containing no plastics or artifical ingredients and it can be served as-is, in a bone-hard form, or microwaved to a biscuit consistency.

swallow the pieces, and die painfully before you realize what is wrong.

All hard natural bones are very abrasive. If your Keeshond is an avid chewer, natural bones may wear away his teeth prematurely; hence, they then should be taken away from your dog when the teething purposes have been served. The badly worn, and usually painful, teeth of many mature dogs can be traced to excessive chewing on natural bones.

Contrary to popular belief, knuckle bones that can be chewed up and swallowed by your Keeshond provide little, if any, usable calcium or other nutriment. They do, however, disturb the digestion of most dogs and cause them to vomit the nourishing food they need.

Dried rawhide products of various types, shapes, sizes, and prices are available on the market and have become quite popular. However, they don't serve the primary chewing functions very well; they are a bit messy when wet from mouthing, and most Keeshonden chew them up rather rapidly—but they have been considered safe for dogs until recently. Now, more and more incidents of death, and near death, by strangulation have been reported to be the results of partially swallowed chunks of rawhide swelling in the throat. More recently, some veterinarians have been attributing cases of acute constipation to large pieces of incompletely digested rawhide in the intestine.

A new product, molded rawhide, is very safe. During the process, the rawhide is melted and then injection molded into the familiar dog shape. It is very hard and is eagerly accepted by

Roar-Hide® is completely edible and is high in protein (over 86%) and low in fat (less than one-third of 1%). Unlike common rawhide, it is safer, less messy, and more fun for your Keeshond.

Keeshonden. The melting process also sterilizes the rawhide. Don't confuse this with pressed rawhide, which is nothing more than small strips of rawhide squeezed together.

The nylon bones, especially those with natural meat and bone fractions added, are probably the most complete, safe, and economical answer to the chewing need. Dogs cannot break them or bite off sizable chunks; hence, they are completely safe—and being longer lasting than other things offered for the purpose, they are economical.

An ideal snack for the Keeshond is the Chicken Chooz™. It is a hard molded bone of chicken and cheese that satisfies the dog's appetite and chewing needs. This is a very high-quality and high-protein product with 70% protein content.

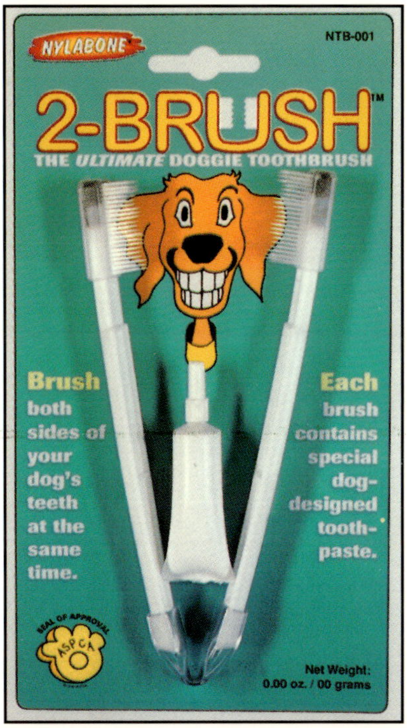

2-Brush™ by Nylabone® is made with two toothbrushes to clean both sides of your Keeshond's teeth at the same time. Each brush contains a reservoir to apply the toothpaste, which is specially formulated for dogs.

Hard chewing raises little bristle-like projections on the surface of the nylon bones—to provide effective interim tooth cleaning and vigorous gum massage, much in the same way your toothbrush does it for you. The little projections are raked off and swallowed in the form of thin shavings, but the chemistry of the nylon is such that they break down in the stomach fluids and pass through without effect.

The toughness of the nylon provides the strong chewing resistance needed for important jaw exercise and effectively aids teething functions, but there is no

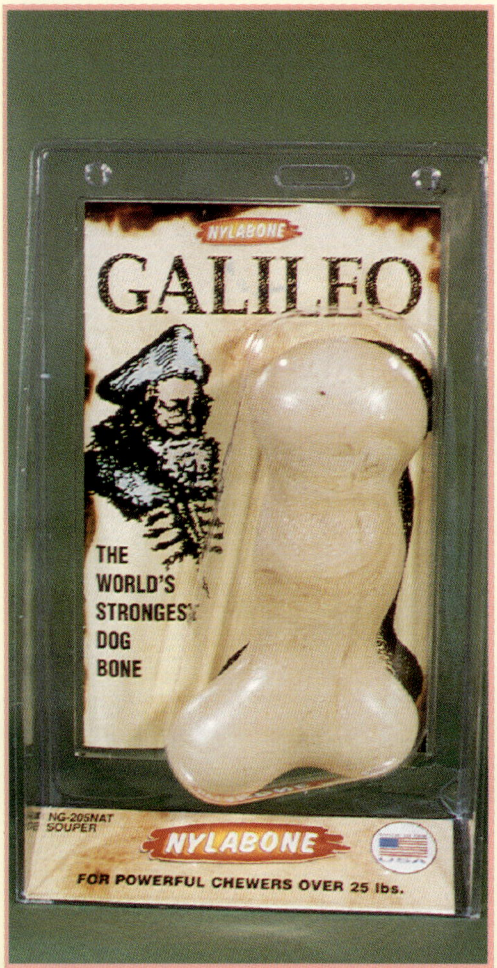

The Galileo™ is an extremely tough nylon pacifier. Its design is based upon original sketches by Galileo. A book explaining the history and workings of the design come inside each package. This might very well be the best design for the Keeshond.

tooth wear because nylon is non-abrasive. Being inert, nylon does not support the growth of microorganisms; and it can be washed in soap and water or it can be sterilized by boiling or in an autoclave.

Nylabone® is highly recommended by veterinarians as a safe, healthy nylon bone that can't splinter or chip. Nylabone® is frizzled by the dog's chewing action, creating a toothbrush-like surface that cleanses the teeth and massages the gums. Nylabone®, the only chew products made of flavor-impregnated solid nylon, are available in your local pet shop. Nylabone® is superior to the cheaper bones because it is made of virgin nylon, which is the strongest and longest-lasting type of nylon available. The cheaper bones are made from recycled or re-ground nylon scraps, and have a tendency to break apart and split easily.

Nothing, however, substitutes for periodic professional attention for your Keeshond's teeth and gums, not any more than your toothbrush can do that for you. Have your Keeshond's teeth cleaned at least once a year by your veterinarian (twice a year is better) and he will be happier, healthier, and far more pleasant to live with.

A chicken-flavored Gumabone® has tiny particles of chicken embedded in it to keep your Keeshond interested in chewing it.

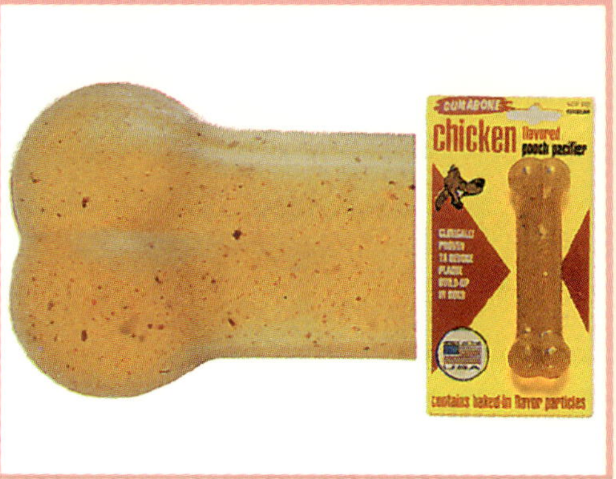

Keeping your Keeshond's coat neat and clean takes a little time, but it is well worth the effort.

GROOMING YOUR KEESHOND

To maintain a healthy and attractive coat, the Keeshond requires daily brushing during the shedding season and weekly brushing thoughout the rest of the year.

One of the best attributes of the Keeshond is his beautiful and extraordinary coat. Typical for a Spitz breed, the Keeshond coat consists of a thick, wooly undercoat with longer guard hairs that give the coat his long, plush appearance. Along with this plush jacket comes a strong need for regular grooming. Unlike short-haired dogs, the Keeshond needs constant attention to his coat if the dog is to look his best. To maintain a healthy and attractive coat the Keeshond requires daily brushing during the shedding season, and weekly brushing is needed the rest of the year.

Grooming your Keeshond does not have to be an unpleasant chore. Instead, this time can be an opportunity to bond with your dog. If your Keeshond learns to enjoy being groomed as a puppy, he will look forward to your grooming sessions together.

To ensure that your Keeshond learns to enjoy grooming at a young age, teach the puppy that brushing, combing and nail clipping is a pleasant experience. Begin by brushing your puppy for short periods of time and then reward him with a game of play or a treat. During the grooming process, be gentle and patient. Let the puppy know that he must stand still and allow you to brush his coat, wipe his face, handle his feet and look at his teeth. Soon your puppy will come to understand that grooming time is an enjoyable experience, one where you pay him a lot of attention!

Grooming also provides an opportunity to get to know your dog's body. While you groom your dog, look for signs and symptoms of health problems. Keep an eye out for growths on the skin, rashes or scabs. Search for fleas and ticks, which can be hard to spot in a Keeshond's thick coat. Look closely at your dog's eyes to make sure they are clear and bright and be on the lookout for ear mites.

Before you begin to groom your Keeshond in earnest, you will need to assemble the right tools. The necessary tools for grooming a Keeshond include a pin brush (a large brush with round-tip pins), a metal-flea comb, a medium-size pair of sharp scissors, nail clippers, a spray bottle filled with water, and a container of styptic powder to help stop any bleeding that may occur if you accidentally cut your dog's nails too short. All of these products can be found in your local pet supply store.

Allow at least half-an-hour per week to groom your Keeshond, and more time if it is shedding season. Find a quiet place with good lighting where you can do your work. Make sure the surface you choose to place your dog is not slippery or uncomfortable for him to stand on. You may even want to consider purchasing a grooming table so you can stand up while grooming your dog. Also,

Grooming should be a joyful experience, as it is time you can spend bonding with your Keeshond.

Grooming provides an opportunity to get to know your Keeshond's body. While you groom, look for signs and symptoms of health problems.

Dogs can pick up parasites from other dogs. Be sure to check your Keeshond's coat thoroughly after he has been around other pets.

choose a place that will make it easy for you to clean up the hair and nail clippings that will be left behind after your grooming session.

Just before you start grooming, lightly spray your Keeshond's body with water from the spray bottle. This will help keep the hair together as you brush it and will eliminate the chance for static electricity to build as you work. Make sure you don't spray your dog in the face with water, as this might register in his mind as something unpleasant associated with grooming.

When grooming your Keeshond, start on one side of the dog near the head and work your way toward the back. Work on one section of coat at a time. Flatten a section of the coat and brush the hair from the skin outwards, using the pin brush. This will enable you to remove excess hair, starting with the double-coat that lays next to the skin, as well as give the fur volume as you brush. Do this all over the dog's body, including on the "trousers," the fluffy hair just above your Keeshond's hocks and elbows.

If you want your Keeshond to have the look typical of a show dog, locate your dog's ruff (the long, thick coat at the base of the neck), and brush it toward his head. This will fluff up the hair and produce the lionish look that Keeshonden are known for.

After brushing your Keeshond's body, work on the shorter hair on his legs and face with the flea comb. As you comb, move in the direction that the hair is growing. (Keep an eye out for fleas, which will get caught in between the teeth of the comb.)

Once your dog has been brushed and combed, you can bring out the scissors to do a little trimming. Before you begin cutting, study some good pictures of Keeshonden so you know what your dog's coat should look like. The purpose of your cutting will be to simply neaten up some of the hair on the dog's legs. Do not go crazy with the scissors or you will destroy the correct look that a Keeshond should have.

Start trimming conservatively around the feet and legs. Loose hairs that stick out from the back of the lower leg can be trimmed, as well as the long tufts of hair that will grow between the dog's toes. (Do not trim the trousers, as

Just before you start grooming, lightly spray your Keeshond's body with water from a spray bottle. This will keep the hair together as you brush it and eliminates the chance for static electricity to build.

these are meant to be long and fluffy.) Your Keeshond's feet should have a rounded look to them, and the scissors will help you achieve this goal.

Once you have finished with the coat, check your Keeshond's nails to see if they need clipping. Dogs that spend a lot of time running on concrete do not need their nails trimmed often, however, if your dog's nails are beginning to curve downward past the level of the foot, they could probably use a trim.

Before you begin trimming, examine the nail to make sure you see the vein that runs through it. You must NOT cut into this vein, because it will cause bleeding and pain to your dog. Instead, cut the part of nail in front of the vein. If you accidentally cut into the quick, as this vein is called, use the styptic powder to stop the bleeding. If you are nervous about cutting your dog's nails for the first time, ask your veterinarian to show you how.

BATHING

Keeshonden are relatively clean dogs and do not have the distinct doggy odor found in many other breeds. Therefore, your Keeshond will not need to be bathed very often. Keeshonden should be washed only when really necessary, to remove mud, excessive dirt or other substances from their coats.

When the time comes to bathe your Keeshond, be sure you have all the items on hand that you will need. Buy a shampoo product that is specifically made for dogs. Be sure you also have some wads of cotton, a soft sponge, a large cup (to pour water on the dog's coat) and a big towel (to dry the dog off).

Before you actually put the dog in the bathtub, groom him first following the instructions above. You may also want to place cotton in your dog's ears to make sure that water doesn't get inside them while you are bathing him.

Fill your bathtub with a few inches of warm water, and place your dog gently into the water. Remember that Keeshonden do not usually like water, so your dog may resist at first. This is where your dog's obedience training can come in handy. Tell your dog to stay and start to pour warm water all over his body, and be careful to avoid wetting his face.

Using the shampoo, start massaging the lather into the dog's coat on the neck, just behind the ears (be careful not to get water in the dog's ears). Lather the dog thoroughly, and be certain to reach all the way through the Keeshond's thick coat to the skin.

Once you have washed your dog, begin the rinsing process. Pour clean, warm water slowly over him in different sections, being careful to remove all of the soap. Several rinsings may be needed to penetrate the Keeshond's thick coat.

Puppies can pick up fleas and ticks from the grass. Be sure to check them carefully after they've been outside.

The Keeshond's coat is high maintenance. Before you bring your Keeshond home, make sure you are prepared to handle the responsibility.

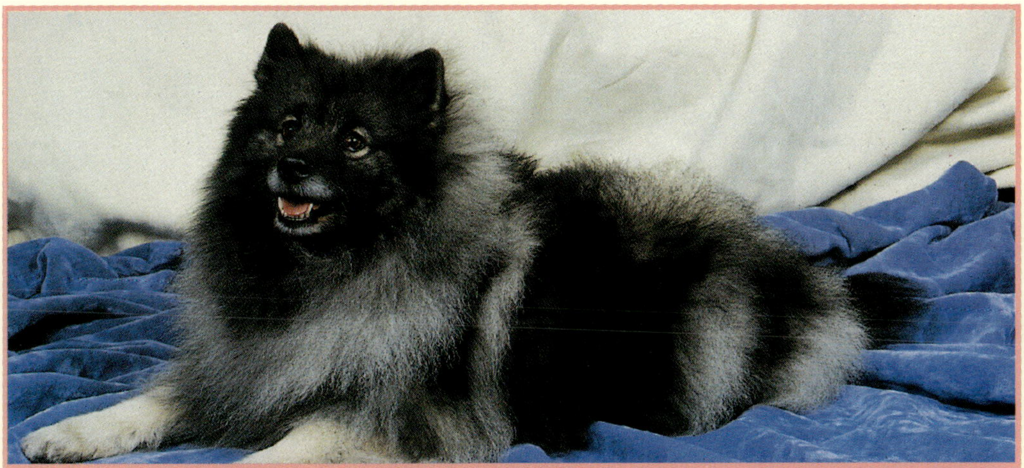

Once your dog is bathed and groomed, you will have a happy, good-looking Keeshond that you will be proud to call yours.

After you have rinsed the dog's body, wash the legs and feet in the same manner, being careful to scrub in between the toes and on the paw pads. Again, rinse these areas very thoroughly, because leftover soap can cause irritation to your dog's skin.

To wash the dog's face, dampen the sponge with soapy water and gently massage the muzzle and cheeks. It is very important not to get soap in your Keshond's eyes, so avoid washing too close to them. If you do accidentally get soap in them, rinse them out with a saline solution made specifically for use in eyes. After washing your dog's face, rinse it off with clear, warm water using the soft sponge.

Once the bath is over, praise your dog and let him know that you appreciate his patience while you washed and scrubbed away. Towel the dog off to remove as much of the water in his coat that you can. If the weather is warm outside, you can let him air-dry outdoors. (Keep in mind that some dogs like to roll in the dirt after a bath, so you may want to keep the dog inside until he is dry to avoid this.)

If there's a chill in the air, keep your dog indoors until his coat is thoroughly dry. Since Keeshonden have such long, thick hair, it may take several hours before your dog is completely dry. Check his coat by reaching your hand all the way to the skin to see if it is dry before you let him outside in cold weather.

Many Keeshond owners use hair dryers to speed up the process of coat drying. The problem with this is that the heat from the hair dryer can damage the Keeshond's coat, and therefore ruin its condition. Air-drying is the preferred method for drying this breed.

Once your dog is bathed and groomed, you will have a happy, good-looking Keeshond that you will be proud to call yours.